# The Carpet Picnic

Written by Clare Helen Welsh

Illustrated by Asma Enayeh

**Collins**

# Ammar and Hanna meet Mel.

# They are having a picnic!

Mel has eggs in her container.

But Ammar has eggs. Hanna has eggs too!

Mel cuts the baps.

Ammar mashes the eggs.
Hanna adds toppings.

But then rain gushes down. Mel sighs.

Ammar thinks.

They picnic on the carpet!

In a week, they meet.

They all pack carrots!

# A picnic

#  Review: After reading

Use your assessment from hearing the children read to choose any GPCs, words or tricky words that need additional practice.

## Read 1: Decoding

- On pages 6 and 7 point to the words **cuts**, **mashes** and **adds**. Ask the children to read each word and then point to the character who is doing the matching action.
- Point to **container** on page 4, allowing the children to sound out and blend. Repeat for **Ammar** on page 5. Then encourage them to read pages 10 and 11 but blend in their heads, silently, before reading the words aloud.

## Read 2: Prosody

- Turn to pages 8 and 9. Point to the speech bubbles. Say: Let's use different voices to read the spoken words. Point out the exclamation marks and say: These mean we must read with extra feeling!
  o Read page 8. Point out how Mel **sighs**. Ask: How do you think Mel is feeling? (e.g. *sad*, *disappointed*)
  o Read page 9 and ask: How is Ammar feeling? (e.g. *excited*) Why? (e.g. *he's thought of an idea*)
- Encourage the children to read the speech bubbles using different voices and tones to show the characters' feelings.

## Read 3: Comprehension

- Ask the children if they would like a picnic, and why. Ask them what sort of food they would have and where they would eat their picnic. Would they enjoy making any of the food in the story?
- Discuss the title of the book. Ask: Why did the children have their picnic on a carpet? (e.g. *because it rained so they couldn't have it on the grass outside*)
- Look together at pages 14 and 15. Using the pictures as prompts, encourage the children to retell the story in sequence.